DAD

THE MAN WHO LIED TO SAVE THE PLANET

12 Timeless Virtues Handed Down to a Son by an Everyday Dad

JAMES MICHAEL PRATT

HEARTLAND BOOKS

For Mom

Published by Heartland Books, Santa Barbara, CA.

Visit the author's web site at www.jmpratt.com

ISBN 1-885027-28-1

Printed in the United States of America

CONTENTS

CONTENTS

INTRODUCTION

For most of his life, my father earned his living and provided for his family through hard, physical labor. Never a rich man, at least not in the way the world looks at wealth and things, he was blessed to see what really mattered and was able to rise above the hardships and privations that he knew as a child and later in life. That is one of the reasons I am so proud of him.

Dad grew up a member of a now much venerated, World War II generation that Tom Brokaw has called "the greatest generation" and which is quickly dying off. The parents of my father's generation were born in the 1800s, and their parents were born before the invention of the steam locomotive

1

and telegraph. That meant my folks and their contemporaries grew up, holding hands with an "old-fashioned" generation of Americans, while witnessing the development of technologies and scientific advancements that would drastically change the way people lived.

My parents therefore occupied a unique place in history: they lived through the modernization of the world but were products of the Victorian age, a bygone era that fostered certain, conservative moral values that were almost universally held by Americans in the early years of the twentieth century.

My parents and their peers were ordinary people who didn't think of themselves as being unique or even particularly admirable. Their lives almost cookie-cutter in every way, they and their neighbors and friends had survived a worldwide economic disaster so encompassing that history books still refer to it as the "Great Depression."

From their modest way of life, from the frontier wisdom that my grandparents knew, from the literal slowness of their modes of transportation, came a code for living and a moral discernment that would serve us well in this day of frenetic schedules, frivolous litigation, unholy political alliances, unbridled media extremes, fast-food merchandising, and communications that take place at the speed of light. What may have seemed ordinary to them yesterday, appears extraordinary to us as we look back with growing envy on their simpler way of life.

I do not suppose that my father, mother, or those of their generation were the last with moral fiber. I do not suppose either that they and their contemporaries were the last to live by the simple truths I will pass along to you in this book. Nor do I suppose that parents of my own generation—the "baby boomers"—or our children, who now are themselves becoming parents, do not possess equivalent values, insights, or moral strengths.

But "the greatest generation" was the last generation to hold hands with the age before indoor plumbing, refrigerators, electric light, radio and television transmission, modern modes of travel, and an ease of life that finally became available to every American household. Dad and those of his generation grew up and lived their lives in harmony, not only with a slower pace of life, but with the values embraced by the founding American families—the immigrants with a dream, who came to our eastern shores seeking religious freedom and liberation from Old World despotism, and moved west to build this nation of ours.

A common wisdom and a certain moral persuasion pervaded the culture of the early twentieth century, which I hope you the reader will recall and find refreshing. I may seem to be eulogizing my father and his peers, but that is simply the result of admiring the values they embraced.

What you are about to read comes from the life of my hero-father, a simple, everyday, blue-collar working man, who was never important to the world at large, who moved dirt with his hands to make a living for most of his adult life—an uncomplicated man, who would be embarrassed by all the fuss I am making over him.

To some, the twelve values and virtues I share as handed down to me may seem new. There are those who may not have had the advantages of a father in the home, a stable family life, and a solid love between parents as I experienced. As I say, my father would be uneasy with all this, but he also would have put his arm around those needing a dad, listened, and then shared a pearl or two of common experience from his times in hopes of helping them along somehow on life's tenuous journey. With those I would especially like to share my dad, the man who lied to save the planet.

CHAPTER 1

HE LIED TO SAVE THE PLANET

D ad descended from pilgrim stock, immigrants who helped found this nation, starting in the mid-1600s. His parents were literally pioneers of the West, hardy folks who embraced traditional moral values—being honest, honoring your promises, working hard, and living virtuous lives—the values that were common to the day and which they tried to pass on to their children and grandchildren.

But now it was 1941, and the fate of the nation so dear to my father and his family, indeed the fate of the world, was about to be decided in the biggest military conflict of all time—the second such global war since the beginning of the young twentieth century.

By December 8, 1941, the day after Japan attacked the United States naval base at Pearl Harbor, our nation was at war, and not just on one front or against just one enemy. Poorly prepared militarily, still using antiquated equipment left over from World War I, and way behind Japan and Germany, whose war machines were already in high gear, the United States joined their allies in a worldwide, desperate struggle to first contain, then drive back the Axis powers.

The task could not have been more daunting. Not since the era of the Roman Legions spreading their military might across the known world had so many countries been conquered in so short a time as those of Europe by Adolph Hitler's well equipped and highly disciplined German forces. In Asia, Japan was on the march, conquering China, Korea, Manchuria, Burma, and the island chains from Malaysia to the deep mid-Pacific. The conquest of the planet by tyrannical and oppressive powers, which were devoid of any mercy for the vanquished, was in full force.

The sneak attack on American installations in Hawaii by Japan, and the subsequent declaration of war by Germany on the United States, galvanized the spirit of freedom across America. It sent our young men flocking to the enlistment stations in every city and county seat in the country.

Their spirits were high, and Uncle Sam, Mom, the girl back home, and even the family dog, were right behind our boys. Our citizens, who turned their lives over to the military to become soldiers, airmen, and sailors, knew that if they didn't stop the enemy on distant shores they certainly would have to do so on our own. They enthusiastically gave themselves to the cause.

Unprepared for such a conflict, still using World War I gear and arms, our young men stepped up to the medical exam tables and accepted whatever uniform was available.

The requirements for enlistment were not too stringent, but minimums were necessary. When our country became threatened during World War II, Dad was under the physical minimum weight to serve in the army.

To enlist in the great cause, my father, Grant

Pratt, had to go against everything he had been taught—he had to tell a lie. He had to "fudge" a bit for a greater purpose. But it was, he would remind me, a "righteous lie"—a lie to save the planet.

"Next," the army sergeant called, pointing to the scale.

Slight of build, if not "skinny," Dad stepped up and onto the platform. "One hundred and twenty pounds," he called out, the minimum weight for passing the physical.

"Pass," the sergeant said. "Take this file to the line over there. Next," the sergeant called out again.

After undergoing basic combat training at Fort Knox, Kentucky, his lying got Dad a free ticket to Ireland for more armored training, and then to North Africa and Italy to join the fight against Nazi Germany and the Italian fascist forces already battling our ally, the British.

Dad later told me that although it wasn't his first lie, it was his biggest. It definitely was bigger than pretending to play the clarinet in the high school band, so that he could get into the Saturday movies for free. It was bigger than saying he didn't know who had smashed several watermelons in a farmer's patch during a "watermelon bust" with friends.

At age twenty-three in 1942, boyish but handsome, and weighing all of one hundred and fifteen pounds, soaking wet, Dad had just lied to make himself available for target practice — to stand in front of the business end of German and Japanese rifles. When he returned home in August of 1944, he weighed one hundred and eighteen pounds. He had actually *gained* three pounds during the war and would laugh, recalling how the army felt so bad about his two years overseas and his "loss of weight" during combat, that they gave him special duty and eventually an early release from the military.

So, he lied. And as kids we were all taught at church where liars go. Along with more than 16,500,000 other Americans who wore the uniform during World War II, he picked up the rifle and went where he was told to go. I wonder if the war would have turned out the way it did if my father had never lied? Perhaps he was the one who tipped the scale in favor of victory.

I guess we will never know. But the point is this: he and his generation were made of stiff stuff—tough material. They had been brought up to "make do or do without." They scrapped and fought their way into work early in life, helping their families by bringing home the pay from their ten- and twelve-hour workdays. They understood teamwork, and after the war, they helped to bring the nation out of the economic slough of the Great Depression.

Tempered in the fires of hard work and war, and their characters molded by the hearth in the homes where they grew up, their mettle stood the test of time. Specific values stand out to those of us who grew up under their guiding hands.

The twelve virtues and values I learned from Dad are also twelve life-lessons that millions of children, now adults my age, grew up learning from their fathers and perhaps even grandfathers, who were from Grant Pratt's time.

Perhaps they weren't any more saints than those before them, but we are missing them now, more than ever. We find ourselves watching helplessly as an average of eleven hundred of those veterans of

World War II pass from us each day. We rightfully feel diminished for not having them near.

While I offer the vignettes and values from my own dad's life, this is a book for all dads today — fathers seeking a way to instill fundamental virtues in their children. It is a "hoorah" for our dads before us and those still with us.

While I offer only what I witnessed about my own dad, this is a tribute to all those who in some way contributed to saving the planet, and it goes without saying, saving the planet was a noble cause, even if it meant lying to help out. But Dad wouldn't have approved of lying under any circumstance other than this, the first of his twelve virtues:

It's okay to lie, but only if you are willing to give your life for it. Otherwise, always tell the truth.

CHAPTER 2

"I SHOULD'VE BOUGHT LAX WHEN IT WAS A BEAN FIELD"

Sometimes we miss out on opportunities that would have enriched us with temporal wealth. A bean field was one such opportunity for Dad. But then Dad thought a lot of what constituted smart business was really just a bunch of "baloney." He viewed things simply and always with the best interest of others in mind. "People are more important than things," he always said.

Whenever I would hear him say that, I would wonder if that wasn't just his way of rationalizing why he never made much money. But I've since come to believe that was how he really felt—that those who spend their lives looking for "easy street" or their "one big break" are foolishly misguided.

"A lot of people spend their entire lives looking for a free lunch, when in fact all they often find is just better baloney—or more of it," he would laugh.

To better appreciate where he was coming from, imagine conditions during the late 1930s and early '40s in Los Angeles, where he graduated from high school and met Mom.

According to Dad, today's Los Angeles International Airport is built on land that was once a bean field. He claimed that he could recall when it was for sale for five dollars per acre.

"Dad?" I asked. "Why didn't you buy it, if it was so cheap?"

"I didn't have five dollars," was his simple response. "Those were depression years. Five dollars was a lot of money back then."

Dad's family was typical of most in those days. Subsistence was a day-to-day affair, and everyone was expected to chip in to help the family survive. They depended on crops from their own home gardens—produce that they used and shared with neighbors. There were no government entitlement programs, no social security safety net, no food stamps or anything else in the form of welfare in those days.

The average American family got by the best they could on a few dollars a week. They didn't expect something they hadn't worked for. Such luxury was for the children of the wealthy class. So they handed down their clothes instead of rushing out to purchase new ones. When a rip or tear occurred, they mended it. Worn shoes were repaired, not discarded. Back then, recycling wasn't a way to save the planet. It was a way to save the family.

"I only made seven dollars a week as produce manager," he would say.

He had come to California in the migration from other farming states, as had many other families suffering hardships during the early years of the Great Depression. When only thirteen years old, he was already a farm worker in the grape fields of the California Central Valley, between Bakersfield and Fresno.

"I worked right along side the Oakies," he would say. It wasn't until later, when I read John Steinbeck's *The Grapes of Wrath* for a college English assignment, that I realized my father had been a participant and first-hand witness to the hard times depicted by the Pulitzer-prize-winning author.

"It was hard back then. But we had our fun, too. And we didn't really know any better," Dad would say. "We just worked together to help the family get by. It was all you could do."

Later, as an Inglewood California High School graduate, he moved up in the world to a produce manager's job at Safeway markets. That was before the war and about the time he met my mother, whose family had also migrated from another state for economic reasons.

Dad was assigned for a time to the small Safeway store (which still stands) on Catalina Island, a tourist destination located twenty-six miles off the Southern California coast.

"We learned that mistakes were costly and there was no one to bail a person out but himself," he told me in recalling how he had once worked two weeks without pay to make up for a blunder he made at the cash register.

A shifty character had come into the store one day and worked a scam on him with a five dollar bill. The man was a fast talker; Dad, admittedly, was not. In fact he always felt most people were thinking too fast for their own good and was often embarrassed that it would take him a minute to thoughtfully digest an idea that others seemed to pick up on quickly.

Not waiting for my Dad to figure out his mental gyrations and sleight-of-hand movements, the crook insisted that Dad had short-changed him from a twenty dollar bill. By the time the con man was through, he had tricked Dad into giving him fifteen dollars from the till. Not until the man had left the store, and Dad had had a chance to think about it, did he realize how the con had worked. The money the cheat got away with amounted to two weeks' wages. Needless to say, Dad never made that mistake again.

Because they were plentiful, beans were the common fare of most people in those days—so much so that a cartoon of the time showed a sad character sitting at the dinner table saying, "Beans, beans, nothing but beans. Beans in the morning, beans in the afternoon, beans at supper time." Who could have foreseen the value of an ordinary bean farm? Or who had $5.00 to invest in an acre of common farm ground?

Paraphrasing Whittier, Dad would chuckle, "Of all sad words of tongue and pen, the saddest are these: it might have *bean*." Or "To *bean* or not to *bean*, that was the question," he would laugh, parodying a line from Shakespeare.

"How was I supposed to know the bean field would turn into an international airport?" he asked.

Those were days of railroad and bus travel. No one but the wealthiest traveled by plane back then. It wasn't until well into the 1950s that air travel began to catch on and international airports were conceived.

Besides, life back in the 1930s and '40s wasn't all about money as it seems to be today. People raised or produced a lot of goods themselves. They worked and played together as families. They expected to do so until the day they died. There weren't investment portfolios, 401Ks, retirement plans, profit sharing, and insurance packages for the common working man and woman. Yes, there were the privileged few and some who simply fared better in business than others, but by and large the average American's expectation was to "use it up, wear it out, make it do, or do without."

"Five dollars could buy a lot of baloney, son. Better to have baloney than beans," he'd say.

It wasn't considered prudent by Dad or most other Californians at the time to pay $5.00 per acre for the bean fields in El Segundo, now the home of LAX. You could grow all the beans a family could eat in your own backyard. As a matter of fact, if you had ventured to buy the bean field, you might have risked the ridicule of your neighbors and friends.

Every now and then I travel to Los Angeles International. As the plane makes its descent and approach from the east you can look out and see Inglewood, the Forum, Hollywood Race Track, and on a clear day, even Catalina Island lying off the blue South Bay coastline.

"Fasten your seat belt, we are headed for a bean field," I've been known to tell the passenger next to me. "See, my dad used to make a dollar a day, and a dollar a day was a lot of money during the Great Depression," I add. "He says he could have bought LAX when it was a bean field. Only five dollars an acre, too." If my seatmate is still listening, I tell him about Dad's other values—the real important ones. "Son," he'd say, "there is just too much baloney in the world, and most things we think are important aren't worth beans. People are more important than things." By this time my fellow passenger is either grinning or can't wait to get away from me.

Dad wasn't able to scrape up the five dollars per acre to buy LAX when it was a bean field, but by virtue of hard work, he did manage to provide many thousands of dollars to finance the rearing of nine children and to pay his way through life.

Now when I fly in to LAX, I see the paved runway approaching, and I smile and think of what he taught; about what really matters most in life. I hear his cheerful voice. Then I whisper almost reverently: "What might have *bean*, Dad."

"Son, people are more important than things. Treat them right. And remember, there is no such thing as a free lunch, just better baloney."

CHAPTER 3

"HOW YA DOIN', CHICKEN?"

One of my fondest memories of my parents' relationship was my father's practice of speaking tender and loving words to my mother.

In the brief birds and bees talk he gave me as I headed into marriage, Dad told me, "I'd rather be a gentleman and receive your mother's love because she wants to give it, than force mine upon her." That really struck me. See, Dad was a *gentle* man by nature, and now I don't think he ever consciously planned or plotted ways to win his wife's affection. He just seemed to always do the right thing by Mom.

When young people marry, they usually have un-realistic expectations about what their relationship will be. Those expectations are spawned in the courtship where each partner is on his or her best behavior. Unless the courtship is lengthy, it's possible that the two starry-eyed people will have seen only the best side of each other prior to the marriage ceremony.

Being newly "in love" prompts a man or a woman to be considerate and thoughtful in an attempt to impress the object of his or her affection. During courtship, gifts are given, courtesy practiced, and tokens of affection frequently exchanged.

Blinded somewhat by excitement and romance, the woman assumes that her man will always be the considerate, gentle, and loving prince she has found. The man is sure that his princess will forever be the sweet, smiling, thoughtful person he discovered while dating. She enters marriage convinced she couldn't have found a more perfect man; he is certain his bride is the most precious thing who ever lived. The embodiment of perfection, each assumes that after they are married, sparks will fly every time they look at each other.

What happens to those sparks after a few years? Where does the perfect man and woman go? Men sometimes complain that their spouse's concern for the children's needs, her professional work, or other interests take precedence over him. She frequently feels that his job, his hobbies and friends, and the pressures of meeting other obligations diminish her importance to him. Often lost in the drudgery of daily routines, there seems to be no room for the romance that originally brought them together, and each mourns the loss of the frequent intimacy of those early married years.

I have had the honor of being entrusted with the precious correspondence my mother and father exchanged while he was away during World War II. In those letters I found a genuinely romantic man and woman, who freely communicated their love, longing, friendship, and fidelity.

There exists in my parents' war-time letters to each other a constant, unabashed expression of adoration between sweethearts. They unselfconsciously addressed each other as "Darling," without any premonition of how terribly sappy it might sound to their children or grandchildren fifty years later. If such expressions are sappy, maudlin, or schmaltzy, as some cynics suggest, then lovers of that era were at the very least a bunch of happy saps.

There is also something honest in those letters that I find enormously appealing. To communicate in those days meant hand writing a letter and believing the postman could deliver it before a month went by or before the soldier died in battle. Written in longhand, great feeling was poured into every carefully chosen word. In our day of easy telephone communication or instant email exchanges, we perhaps can't imagine the thrill it must have been to receive such a letter or the excitement with which lovers in my parents' generation pored over the words, savoring each expression of affection, longing for the reunion that seemed so far off and uncertain.

You may think I am romanticizing all of this — that a chaste love affair such as I have described my parents having is idealized or improbable. I don't believe so. See, they had something largely lost to us now; shining armor still existed. There is a certain appealing flavor to the mutual adoration found in their letters and in speech; an unhurried and tender part of courtship was the manner in which they communicated from the heart—the knight to his lady, the lady to her knight.

Watch any romantic movie made in the 1930s, '40s, or '50s. The screenwriters turned out wonderful love stories, without explicitly depicting sex. Limited by industry codes and the mores and standards of the time, filmmakers found a way to create love scenes that left much to the imagination and in many ways generated more passion than today's blatant and gratuitous dramatizations. Filmmakers then could never have imagined doing what their counterparts of today are permitted to do. To audiences of my parents' generation, it would have not been real, and in fact moviegoers would have been embarrassed by the vulgarity of it all.

That is not to say my parents' generation were all saints, were all perfect, or that there wasn't such a thing as sexual promiscuity in those days. It obviously has always existed, but it was not generally condoned or glamorized, and when it was portrayed in the movies, it wasn't graphically shown. There was still such a thing as the depiction of guilt and resulting consequences for choices. That was a reflection of the mores and standards most Americans embraced. They were, and those still with us are, to their credit, great romantics.

Why I find the brand of love and romance of my parents' era so appealing might be more easily understood if I share, as Paul Harvey says in his daily radio monologue, "the rest of the story."

Having found each other, my parents had to endure two and a half years of wartime separation before they could marry. They kept their romance alive through written correspondence, which only increased their desire for each other. Dad revealed to me that he was as excited as any man to experience the intimacies of marriage but that he and Mom had waited until after they were married. Contrary to the way things are often done these days, they exercised restraint and patience in order to do it right, according to the expectations of their day.

That kind of morality was not uncommon in those times, and it helped lay the foundation for enduring marriages.

As I reflect on my parents' relationship and recall Dad's considerate treatment of Mom, I realize that his conduct was deeply rooted in the culture of those times. He was conditioned to be patient and gentlemanly, she to be demure and chaste.

Contrast that with our current situation. We live in a world where instant gratification is the thing and where we demand *drive-through* convenience, *fast-food* service, and *express* check-out lanes. Computers enable us to retrieve data instantly, expedite our purchases, and communicate in the flickering of an eye. Most of us are unwilling to wait for *anything*.

We live at a pace that my folks and their friends could never have imagined. They grew up and lived in a time where most bread was still hand-kneaded at home, television was yet unborn, radio was limited to a couple of stations, cars rarely traveled over fifty miles per hour, music was Crosby and Sinatra crooning, and Mabel at the phone company still connected you at reverse warp speed. The "EAT GAS FOOD" signs along America's highways, encouraging you to stop your car, only signaled the beginning of the modern age where you could do more than one thing in one place.

It was against that backdrop that Dad wooed

Mom and in which he tapped into the secret that kept their love alive. Dad wasn't book-trained or college-bred, but he intuitively knew the everyday things he could do to make Mom happy.

After I had married, I once turned to Dad for some advice. Some of the magic my wife and I had discovered in each other while dating had diminished, and I wondered how I could rekindle some of that. As muddle-brained as any man, I was missing the great secret.

I don't think my father stopped and thought: "Now I am going to hit that son of mine right between the eyes with a profound statement on the subject of loving a woman, one he will never forget."

What he said was this: "Son, your mother knows I love her because no matter what each day brings, I try to tell her so and show that I do by listening. Just treat her like you did back when you thought she was perfect." Then he taught me the great truth:

"Son, just adore her, and everything will be fine."

He somehow understood that after dating, after

courtship, and after marriage, a woman still desires to be *adored*.

The wisdom was just good old-fashioned philosophy from his day, and it still works.

I'd gotten terribly busy with life. My wife had, too. We were on a frenzied pace to save the world, our local church, the kids' soccer team, the PTA, and the elementary school from disaster but had forgotten about this *adoration* thing. See, to adore someone takes time and effort, the same kind of time and effort we had invested during our dating years. Dad was reminding me of something I had forgotten.

Adoring the girl he married was the finest thing Dad ever did for Mom, and it was one of the finest things he did for us seven boys. It is a lesson I am understanding with clarity only now.

Webster's defines *adore* as: 1. To worship as divine 2. To love or honor greatly; idolize 3. To like very much. To be adored is more than receiving flowers or gifts, although those certainly are ways to remember the person you love.

Often, after the five of us boys under sixteen years old had pushed our mom to the brink of tears, after we had her wagon surrounded and she felt she was just about to take the last arrow, my father would walk in from work. Tired and dirty from a hard day's labor in construction, he would look at my frazzled mother, take her in his arms, and say, "How ya doin', chicken?"

Never mind that he carried the odor of manual labor, dust and sweat still clinging to him, she was willing to be held. There was an embrace, eye contact that invited her to ventilate her frustration, and a confirmation of her worth. Dad not only physically shielded her from our antics but also met her emotional needs. That, I have come to know, was a major part of their intimacy.

Dad probably couldn't have articulated it, but he intuitively practiced what Henry Ward Beecher, nineteenth century author and preacher, taught: "Do not keep the alabaster boxes of your loves and tenderness sealed up until your friends are dead. Fill their lives with sweetness. Speak approving, cheering words while their ears can hear them and while their hearts can be thrilled by them."

I doubt there exists more precious words in any language than the simple three, "I love you." I certainly cannot hear them enough. Spoken by my wife, my daughter, my son, my brothers, sisters, and friends—those three words give meaning to life and are always thrilling to hear.

"How ya doin', chicken?" might not sound like "I love you," or "Darling, I adore you," but Mom knew. It was their little code.

What Dad taught me when I was struggling in the early years of my marriage to understand the secrets of a good one—one as strong as he and Mom had achieved—was this:

Son, just adore her, and everything will be fine.

CHAPTER 4

THE GOOD HUMOR MAN

Science has proven that laughter is good for you. Medical studies have shown that laughter creates pleasure, causing endorphins to cruise through our bodies, creating a euphoria not unlike a drug-induced high. Medicine has further shown that humor and laughter reduce levels of stress, lower the blood pressure, and reverse symptoms of headache and other pain.

The book of Proverbs, chapter 17, verse 22 reads: "A merry heart doeth good like a medicine; but a broken spirit drieth the bones."

Laughter rejuvenates body and soul. The *Readers' Digest's* popular "Laughter Is the Best Medicine" section provides a monthly testimonial that gut-busting humor can work miracles. In short, laughter and having a good sense of humor are good medicine.

My dad had a well-cultivated sense of humor. His wit contributed much to the pleasant atmosphere in our home and family.

Growing up in Southern California in the 1950s and early '60s, one of the things we kids looked forward to was the daily arrival of the Good Humor Man in our neighborhood. When we heard the familiar music of his truck, the challenge was to get five or ten cents from our parents to buy one of his frozen treats — Popsicles, Good Humor Bars with chocolate coating on the outside and vanilla ice cream on the inside, and snowcones. The appearance of the Good Humor Man was as dependable as the schedule of daily TV shows: *Captain Kangaroo, The Lone Ranger, Superman,* or *Popeye.*

I didn't realize until much later in life how much the Good Humor truck driver and my Dad had in common. You never found a grouch behind the wheel of the ice cream truck, and no matter how tired or worn out, you never found a grouch when dealing with Grant Pratt. I think his native cheerfulness was a gift, a personality trait that some people are born with and the rest of us have to learn.

"Son, don't forget to laugh. A good sense of humor will win every time. Share it with others," he reminded me with a smile when on a particularly serious crusade, I was scheduled to speak and try to sell an idea to a large audience.

During the first twenty years of my life, Dad worked as a manual laborer, moving dirt with his "skiploader" tractor in the post-war construction boom of the times. Had he not been so employed, I can easily picture him happily driving the Good Humor ice cream truck, playing the chiming song, becoming friends with all the children, and offering that perpetual, friendly smile, the grin he was so famous for.

There was no work that was beneath Dad. He believed all worthy endeavors to be honorable, so I say that I could see him doing that ice cream route job in that spirit. He would have found a way to make it fun.

As I look back, Dad was our very own Pratt family "good humor man." One liners came easily.

Corny jokes were stored in his mind in the way some people store factoids, statistics, or other information.

"Son," he would say as we worked together, "a rooster followed his favorite hen across the dirt road everyday. The rooster always puffed up his chest and offered a loud 'cock-a-doodle-do' when they safely got across the road. One day the hen asked why he never wrote love notes to her. So the rooster stopped in the middle of the road and pecked out a love note to the hen in the dirt as a fast moving, pickup truck sped toward him. He finished the love note just seconds before becoming a hood ornament on the truck. What did the hen say as the truck continued on down the road?"

"I don't know, Dad. What did the hen say?" I would oblige.

Dad would try to hide his grin, proud of having created a good punch line, and pausing as good joke meisters do.

"Cock-a-doodle-did," he'd chuckle.

The sheer enjoyment he took in telling what today's youngsters would call "old people jokes" was what made me laugh. "Son . . ." he'd say, and go on to the next joke, if I laughed hard enough to encourage him.

Dad never told "off-color" stories or jokes that disparaged a race or an individual. And he wouldn't listen with approval to stories that made fun of people or had any sexual overtones. He possessed a certain dignity, and his humor was definitely "G-rated."

As I write this, I am not sure I know three jokes, total—corny or not. My favorites are attorney jokes, but I still can't seem to make the punch lines come out right. Timing is important, and Dad had timing down. I try, but to no avail. I apparently didn't draw a "good humor" gene from the Pratt heredity pool.

In the movie *Good Morning, Vietnam,* the actor Robin Williams portrays a comedic armed forces radio personality who enjoys a brilliant but abbreviated career. Dismissed from his job by his uptight superior officer, who does not like Williams or his brand of freewheeling humor, Williams declares that the arrogant lieutenant wouldn't know good humor if he heard it.

Nevertheless, the lieutenant takes over the

microphone himself, delivering a daily diet of staid and corny jokes and demonstrating his total lack of comedic timing or mastery. When called on the carpet for dismissing Williams and then botching the job himself, the arrogant lieutenant defends himself by saying, "General, sir, just for the record, I want it to be noted that in my heart, I know I am a funny man."

Well, I know in my heart I'm *not* a funny man, but I think I have a good sense of humor. If so, I attribute that to being raised by Grant Pratt, a man who religiously read the funny pages of the Sunday newspaper. I never saw him read any news section of the daily or Sunday paper, but he thoroughly enjoyed reading the comics. They were, to him, the most meaningful section of any newspaper because they put forth great issues of life in light and humorous terms.

"Funny Page" readers are a special breed. I admit that I have read the Sunday comics maybe a dozen times in my life, but I read the daily newspaper, and did as a child, in a very thorough manner. Comics seem so senseless to a hard-news type like me.

I've never really understood why my kids admonish me to "lighten up." *In my heart I know I can be funny,* I think to myself.

Once, during a rather lengthy trip by car, to the amazement of my family, I succumbed to spontaneity. I spied a county fair off the road during one of our pit stops in northern Utah on the way to grandma's house in Idaho. I don't understand what my children and their lighthearted mother see in standing in lines at amusement parks for a few seconds of being twirled around, tossed, or rocketed to the sky in some man-made slingshot; but I figured it would make me popular with them if I sprang for twenty bucks for a few rides and an hour out of the car.

How bad can it be? This is a safe, nonalcoholic, small-town fair, I reasoned. I must admit, I am not a fan of carnival rides and the type of grungy personnel who often man them. But I let reason fly and entered the world of garish lights, carnival barkers, and attractions such as the Tilt-a-Whirl, Ferris wheel, and miniature roller coaster—rickety rides that looked as reliable as the worn-out, tired, rattle-traps we out west call "desert Cadillacs."

You know the type of car — the one that has gray primer patches all over, long fin-style rear wheel wells, fenders tied to the car with baling wire, some indefinable GM brand from the 1960s or 1970s, and dust swirling around it as it speeds down a country road or passes you on the highway somewhere in the neighborhood of ninety miles an hour, only to come to a screeching halt at the first sign of a convenience store.

Anyway, carnival rides remind me of that type of moving chariot, and the ride operators seem to be the owners of most desert Cadillacs extant.

I immediately became uneasy, wondering what I was doing there, late at night, without a sidearm to protect my family. Tattooed people with silver studs in their tongues and an assortment of other rings worn in their noses, eyebrows, and ears now surrounded me.

"Where did northern Utah go?" I whispered into my wife's ear.

"What?" she asked, giving me one of her will-you-calm-down-and-have-some-fun! looks.

"You know. Where did all these weirdos come from?"

"Oh, hush!" she replied as we continued through the crowd to the ticket booths.

"Twenty bucks and we're outta here!" I said and handed over a twenty dollar bill to the ticket seller.

We had entered another world, a world of strange looking and acting people, a world that might have been out of a 1950's sci-fi movie. You know, the small-rural-town-taken-over-by-aliens-from-another-planet type of movie. The kind of flick where the townspeople walk zombie-like from ride to ride, looking as though their brains have been sucked out and they have become utterly senseless.

I was relieved to see a few armed deputies circulating through the crowd. It was also a comfort to see a number of "normal looking" people enjoying the rides and playing the midway games, and I reminded myself that this was, after all, just amusement. Though I am not one of them, lots of people apparently love to be twirled, spun, and made dizzy.

I tolerated the amusement for about as long as I could, waiting impatiently for my family to use up the tickets so we could escape the noise and babble of the carnival. Ignoring my negative feelings, and ignorant of the danger I saw all around us, my family happily went from one ride to another, until we reached the main attraction: The *Gravitron!*

Have you ever seen one? It is a silver disk—a flying saucer-looking type of contraption that holds up to fifty people and travels at a rate that would get you a speeding ticket on the highway. It opened its giant maw and swallowed my children. Amy and Mike, my only hope of future progeny, disappeared smilingly into its bowels and were now completely at the mercy of the alien at the controls.

I turned to my wife. "Jeanne, I don't think this is such a good idea. I mean, how responsible is it to put your kids in the hands of that guy and let him spin them around until they are mush-brained? This is insane!"

"Oh, lighten up and let them have some fun," she replied.

"Let them have some fun," I muttered to myself. "Plastered against the wall of some rattletrap ride, spinning at sixty miles per hour, probably puking their guts out," I grumbled. "I must be crazy," I complained against myself, convinced I had abdicated my duty as the guardian and protector of my children's safety.

After several long minutes, to my relief, the kids emerged, grinning as they had upon entering. "Hey, Dad, can we do that again?"

"No!" I barked. They had survived once, and I wasn't about to give the operator another shot at my kids. "Dad never would have allowed this," I grumbled. *Or would he?* I answered myself. Dad was a lighthearted guy. A fun guy. *Yeah, but he was from an earlier, less-complicated, safer time and wouldn't understand the current dangers like I do,* I argued with myself.

See, my Dad was old. From another time zone. Out of touch. And he read the comics. What could you expect of a man who derived such pleasure and whose entire view of the world was gained through reading the funny pages of the Sunday newspaper?

Occasionally, Dad would be heard chuckling and then would go looking for some scissors. Comic strips found their way into his wallet and as bookmarks into the only other books he read with regularity, his scriptures.

I left the dusty carnival, as fast as my feet could

lead us, to the slaps on the back and the congratulations of my family for having let my hair down a bit. "Yeah, yeah!" I replied. "Let's get out of here before the body snatchers get me, too."

Not long after that, I caught my then nineteen-year-old son, Mike, reading the Sunday newspaper. It was Monday now, and he was sprawled out on the couch, holding the newspaper up in front of his face. I was impressed. *Catching up on the news. About time he begins to take life more seriously,* I thought. It was one of those rare moments where a parent takes real pride in a son's progress toward responsible adulthood.

Mike's a lot like his Grandpa Pratt: kind, generous, fun-loving, but not too heavy into serious or world events, a good person who probably won't ever develop ulcers. Now he was actually reading the newspaper, too.

I soon discovered he wasn't nearly as concerned about what the world was doing, as I had hoped. He looked up at me and said he had a craving for a large shrimp platter, so I offered.

"Come on. Let's go to the Red Lobster."

The look "really?" crossed his face and I nodded,

grabbed the car keys, and motioned for him to follow. I saw it as one of those opportunities where a son would be trapped and have to listen to the wisdom of his father—an opportunity to give guidance, some real powerful stuff!

So we went to dinner, and I started my lecture while we were waiting for our food. I was trying to explain that now that he would soon be turning twenty, there were things I expected of him, some decisions about career and life that would need to be made, and how he needed to set some long-term goals. I explained in the clearest of terms how present world affairs would probably decide his fate if he didn't decide it first.

"Do you understand what I am telling you?" I asked.

He looked up from his shrimp plate with a blank stare and asked, "About what?"

I shook my head, chuckled, and thought, *If that isn't justice.* Had I really listened to my father at that age? Does anyone?

When we got home, I picked up the Sunday paper my son had been looking at to see if he had been into some serious reading. I was looking for any reason to have hope. I smiled and laid the paper down. The "funny page" section was worked inside the hard news section and had been my son's earlier source of contemplation.

The "good humor" gene may have skipped a generation in me, but it was alive and well in my boy. I chuckled, and a vision of my father crossed my mind. "The Good Humor Man," I whispered.

"Son, don't forget to laugh. A good sense of humor will win every time."

CHAPTER 5

"IT'S BETTER TO BE KIND THAN TO BE RIGHT"

My dad lived by an unwritten motto: "It's better to be kind than to be right." That's what he said to me one day as I voiced resentment over the way a customer had treated him in our small, family-owned, country retail store.

For Dad, the effects of kindness were always more important than the results of justice. I admit, by the time I dropped out of college to help him run his floundering store business, I was tired of all the times I had seen others renege on promises made to him or refuse to pay him for goods delivered or services rendered. I was aware of situations that went back twenty years where Dad simply forgave people their debts to him, as if he could afford to do so.

It is one thing to be wealthy and have the financial wherewithal to forgive debts, but it is another to be constantly on the verge of being unable to make a living for a large family or meet your own obligations, then forgive what someone else owes you. I had decided, by the time I rode in from college to the rescue, I wasn't going to allow Dad to get beat up financially anymore.

The closest I ever saw my Dad come to demanding justice was when a couple of steers he had boarded at a local caretaker, a ranch of sorts, were "rustled" by the ranch manager, who Dad and Mom caught in his lie. I thought a hanging might take place, but Dad stopped Mom.

With my boyish imagination I was eager to see the man swing from the short end of a rope. In the antiquated California law of the 1960s, cattle rustling was still punishable by hanging, and we lived near Corriganville, a movie backdrop built originally by stunt man "Crash" Corrigan. It later became known as Hopetown when Bob Hope purchased the replica of an 1870s western town. With its false-front stores and dusty streets, it was the site of Rin Tin Tin's *Fort Apache* and so many other "B" westerns made in the 1940s and '50s.

There was a suitable oak tree there and a good audience every weekend, too—tourists who came to see the staged gunfights and stunt performances. I reasoned a hanging would have played out well, and nobody but the judge and the lawyers, Mom and Dad, and of course, the cattle rustler, would have to know it wasn't a stunt after all.

Justice, this time, I thought.

But justice didn't prevail. Lack of evidence (the cattle by then had been reduced to hamburger patties in some drive-through restaurant) was the reason the charges were dismissed. I remember my parents' disappointment over the loss of the money and the steers and how angry they were at the lying, cheating, modern-day cattle thief. As far as I know, that was the only time Mom and Dad ever tried to use the law to settle a dispute. When it didn't work out in their favor and it became clear that injustice would win out, they simply forgave the offense and moved on with life.

I learned a valuable lesson as I watched my father

repeatedly forgive those who, through the course of his life, would wrong him, take advantage of him, or in business fail to keep agreements with him.

In his own way, Dad simply believed that remaining angry, bearing a grudge, or working to get even could never result in peace of mind, contentment, or the quality of kindness. "Being right doesn't give you the right to get even. Kindness wins every argument, Son," he'd say. "Getting angry will just cost you time, money, and energy and only make you bitter." He believed this to be true in all situations, but especially when you were "right."

Dad lived as the Swiss philosopher and poet, Henri Frederic Amel, had suggested:

> Life is short and we have never too much time for gladdening the hearts of those who are traveling the dark journey with us. Oh, be swift to love, make haste to be kind.

Dad was an active churchgoer. Because of his ability to get along with people, he was often given assignments by his church leaders to look up the most ornery people — the most recalcitrant and difficult members on the church's roll.

I remember going with him once to the home of a particularly difficult member. The older lady had let it be known she wanted no visitors. She lived in a weathered cottage on a hillside, in a spooky area of town known to have more belligerents per capita than any other neighborhood in Ventura County. People who liked their privacy and wished others would leave them alone had found it an agreeable place to live.

I knew that neighborhood. I'd had my first job there, delivering newspapers. It was the summer of 1962, and you had to be officially ten years old to be a *Los Angeles Herald Examiner* paperboy. I was only nine that year, but following my dad's World War II example, I had lied (about my age) to get the job—a job no one else apparently wanted. The subscribers found it easy to turn away a young paperboy seeking to collect their bill. Each of them also had a dog—never a little pooch, always a huge mastiff—one that could take a man's leg off. Given that and the steep dirt roads I had to push my bike up in the hilly Santa Susana Knolls part of town, I felt God might forgive my lie.

Working seven days a week, I made only $22.00

over three months. To this day I can tell you which houses I had and how big the dogs were.

Many summers passed, then Dad got his church visiting assignment, to call on the cranky old woman living in the dark cottage on the hill. I remembered her. In my nine-year-old mind, she was the "witch" I dreaded seeing. Now justice was being served for me telling a lie. I was to be Dad's companion and would have to endure this cheerfully.

As we pulled into the crumbling asphalt drive one hot day in 1967, I warned Dad about the dog and told him what the lady was like. It seems to me he just mumbled something like, "Well, we'll see."

I'll never forget the amazing transformation in that old lady in the presence of my soft-spoken father. She tried but couldn't seem to muster up a yell, or a threat, or a loud voice at all, just: "Since you're here anyway, you might as well come in." I raised an eyebrow at the dog and kept my eye on him. He didn't seem like the same dog I had known years before. But of course he was an old, tired dog by now.

We had to down some hard cookies and a glass of juice or fruit punch of some kind while she did most of the talking. In his inimitable, friendly way, Dad just smiled, and let her go on. By the end of our visit, she was saying what a good conversationalist and nice man Dad was.

She never came back to church but always let Dad in to visit. She often said, "Grant Pratt is the only person I'll accept from that church."

The day of Dad's memorial service, I thumbed through the thin onionskin pages of his personal Bible. Read often by him, it was also where he kept private notes and various clippings from the funny papers—comic strips that described the human condition in a way he understood.

I wasn't searching for anything specific, just something that would connect me with him. I noted the underlined passages and smiled at some of the clippings. There were also some well-worn, 3 X 5 index cards, written in his hand with blue fountain pen ink. One of them contained a quotation from an unknown author:

> I shall not pass through this world but once. Any good thing, therefore, that I can do, or any kindness that I can show to any

human being, let me do it now. Let me not defer it or neglect it, for I shall not pass this way again.

Today, I carry those tattered and worn index cards in the pages of my own Bible. Perhaps my son or daughter will find them one day, and the tradition will go on.

Kindness. It was more than just a word to Dad. It was something he practiced daily. To those who knew him, his life was a silent sermon made up of the many quiet acts of charity and service he rendered to others. He lived a successful life based on a couple of simple notions: "Treating people kindly takes the wind out of the sail of the most ornery," and "It is always better to be kind than to work to prove you are right."

He'd be embarrassed for me to be making such a big deal out of some of his sayings and ways. But those who knew him well will agree with me that his life was a sermon lived, and its title was:

"It's better to be kind than to be right."

CHAPTER 6

"IF IT IS CONVENIENT, IT PROBABLY ISN'T SERVICE"

You see, Son, service isn't about me, it's about them."

"I say it's about you. Look how you drop everything to go off and help someone. Sure it helps them, but what do you get out of it?" I responded with boyish prodding.

I was seventeen years old, and Dad and I were having this philosophical debate over why we had to go down to the "old barn," as we called it, and spend three or four hours working on our church's newspaper recycling project.

We would take all the papers people donated and store them in a weather-beaten barn on land the church had purchased for use in constructing a new building. There was this bundling machine in the barn that we'd load with the week's gathered papers. At just the right height, a hydraulic powered masher would come down and compress the papers into a bale similar in size to a bale of hay. Then with the same kind of wire used to bale hay, we'd tie the bundle off, snip the extra wire, and stack the bundles on pallets. If a long flatbed truck was there to take them to the recycling plant, we'd form a line and toss the bales by the hundreds onto the truck. The money earned was to be used to help construct a new meetinghouse.

I recall that it was almost always the same men who would show up. All old guys, it seemed to me. Oh, there were a few teens like me, and some in their twenties, like my two older brothers, Grant and Nick, a few more in their thirties, but mostly some really old guys like my dad, who were in their late forties or early fifties. I know for sure Dad was the oldest. I wondered why Dad never seemed to resent the fact that only the same men always showed up.

I wasn't too thrilled to be using my after-school nights for this "service" project, but I couldn't figure out how I could, in good conscience, let Dad, an old guy, go off after a long day in construction to do more manual labor while I stayed home. The bales were heavy. We'd sweat and grunt and be tired at the end. After loading a few hundred bales, all we'd earned was a soda pop and a pat on the back.

I recall thinking, *How do they do it? These old guys? I know how I do it. I'm seventeen, a weight-lifting, high-school football player. I'm young. But I can barely keep up. And they are joking around and laughing, like this is fun or something.*

Years later, living as a college drop-out in order to help Dad out in his country store, I recalled that earlier project and was commenting on it and the hundreds of service projects Dad had joined in since.

We had just unloaded a truckload of one-hundred-pound sacks of grain and were sitting next to each other on the tailgate of a twenty-foot bobtail truck, drinking a soda and cooling down. Dad was now in his mid-to-late fifties, and I was amazed at his strength and endurance.

I was in a bit of a negative mood. "We've done

a lot of things for free. It's no wonder we were always broke," I complained.

"Things always come back to you how you send them out," he reminded me.

"Dad, if so, where's the money?"

"It's not always about money," he answered simply.

"What, then?"

"Doing a good job. Keeping your word. Helping folks out," he replied.

"You're never going to be a rich man with that attitude," I laughed. I was twenty-two. I understood these things.

"Maybe not. But I sleep well at night. And besides, we're doing some good."

"Oh," I agreed as if convinced.

"Let me tell you a story, Son. There was this day I brought the skip-loader home to do some grading on our lot down on Christine Avenue. You know how I worked a lot of six-day weeks back then."

"Still do," I grunted.

"Well," he continued, ignoring my grumbling, "there was this one Saturday I went to considerable trouble to get the tractor home from the job site.

And as soon as people from the church found out I had the tractor, they started calling on the phone. 'Grant, you suppose you could even out my backyard for me?' Then a neighbor would see me, and I'd be doing his garden.

"After about four of those service opportunities it was getting late into the afternoon. I had finally gotten the tractor home and was starting on our place when the phone rang. It was my good friend John. He started out by saying, 'Grant, if it wouldn't be inconvenient, I was wondering if you could come over and help me on my yard with that tractor of yours.'

"I was a bit perturbed by this time but remembered something I was taught long ago. I answered, 'Brother John, it is inconvenient, but if it was convenient, it wouldn't be service. I'll be right over.'"

Dad finished. There was a long pause.

"So what's the moral?" I finally asked, knowing all along what it was, just not knowing how he would put it.

He explained the basic Bible teaching, that service to others is one of the basic creeds that a civilized society orders itself by. That without service to others, we would all live in a shell of selfishness, greed, envy, and pride.

I nodded and understood something of the kind of man my father was. I wondered if I could ever possibly match him and realized that I probably never would. I had always been too stubborn, too opinionated, and too justice-oriented in my life. The age-old aphorism "it serves them right" had been useful to me in the past. Old habits die hard.

But then again, I had seen a lot of service too by then; a lot of volunteering without the coercion I had felt applied in my youth. I had, since the age of nineteen, been trying to strip off the "old man"— no, not my dad, but the selfish, self-serving youth I had been.

I had given up two years of my life, college-age years, to go to a foreign land and preach, serve, and help other people—people I didn't know. They had turned out to be the two happiest years of my life. I wondered, *Why is it that when you are so wrapped up in giving something—time, energy, means—to others, it makes you so happy?* I had never been happier, ever. And at that time I was all of twenty-two as I listened to the wisdom my father put into a context I could finally understand.

We sat together on the tailgate of the truck, sipping the last of our sodas. I had given up college for this, too, to be here helping Dad. I had some regrets about it, probably felt a little sorry for myself, certain that what I had done was not a good career move. Even so, I was generally at peace. Dad had misunderstood my motive, thinking I had a compelling interest in working in the family business. But that wasn't it. I needed to give something back, and I needed to be with him when he needed it most.

I thought back on the time I had spent in South America, recalling the hundreds of miles walked, the thousands of doors I had knocked on, the physical labor that had been given, the prayers I had offered, and the tears I had shed during the time I had served as a minister in that foreign land.

"It's always made you happy, hasn't it, Dad?"

"What's that?"

"You know. Service."

"Yes," he replied simply.

"It's made a difference, Dad."

"Oh, I don't know," he replied modestly.

"Your sons saw. Your daughters, too. And, Dad, there's no telling how far that will reach."

"Thanks, Son," he quietly said, with a gentle pat on my back.

I thought I caught a hint of moisture in his eye and detected a catch in his voice.

I took a ride in my car, alone, that night. I recall getting misty-eyed, thinking about the poor people in Peru and the hundreds of homes I had entered and the thousands of hours I had given there. *Had I made a difference?* I wondered. Even if I hadn't changed anyone else, I was still the winner. Service had changed me.

See, Dad had this long view of life. "If it is convenient, then it probably isn't service," he always said. I have never forgotten that simple declaration. I have never forgotten how Dad was always there, no matter how unfair it seemed, no matter whose turn to serve it really was. That ready and willing nature to give may have exhausted him, but then he was always so happy.

Was that it after all? Bread cast on the water? You get back what you send out?

Those times, lean years, when I thought I was sacrificing my schooling and career training to help him, mean the world to me now. No business course could have taught me more about the fundamentals of making customers happy, more about the basics of treating others generously.

I don't think about the paper drives much anymore, but when I do, I am more amazed than ever that the "old man" could not only keep up with us younger men and teens but outlast us if he had to.

I am his age now, the age he was when together we threw hundreds of bales of newspapers onto semitrailers and when we lifted endless one-hundred-pound sacks of grain into a truck at the store on the Santa Susana Pass Road. Every now and then, when I look into the mirror, I swear that I can see Dad looking back at me.

He smiles, I smile back and nod, and then get misty-eyed and leave the mirror to go about my daily tasks. I hear his voice, though:

You see, Son, if it's convenient, it probably isn't service.

CHAPTER 7

"THERE'S NO SUBSTITUTE FOR A GOOD NAME"

When you give a man your word, you've got to keep it. A good name never dies," my dad often told me.

Intellectually that was an easy one.

Honor, trust, good faith, are still principles that make all kinds of enterprises work. But there was a time when you just "gave a man your word," and it was as good as any written contract. What that meant to most people of my dad's generation is this: *Your name is only as good as your word. You fail to keep your word, and you permanently tarnish your name.*

Dad was extremely proud of the Pratt heritage. He never tired of recalling that we had come from sturdy pioneer stock. As kids, we were often reminded that in 1847, Great-grandfather Parley P. Pratt had walked across the plains, all the way from the Mississippi River to the Rocky Mountains. Before that, in the 1830s, he had sailed to England, and in the 1850s he'd gone to Chile, both times in the name of God.

"Can't put a price on a good name. A good name will open doors for you," Dad always said.

"How come the Pratts are all broke?" I asked once. As a young man, I equated success with wealth. It's a common thing to do, I suppose.

He laughed and told me again about Parley's Canyon, which was named after Great-grandfather Parley P. Pratt. He reminded me that in pioneer times, Parley had built the first tollroad in Utah through that canyon. It was a potentially lucrative enterprise, since that was the route used by anyone trying to get to Salt Lake City from Park City or Wyoming or anyplace east of there. Today, Interstate Highway I-80 follows that same route.

"It doesn't make sense, Dad. How come he gave the tollroad up?" I asked. I knew Brigham Young had kept him constantly traveling in and out of the Utah Territory on a succession of assigned missions, but that wasn't the reason. Parley had plenty of sons who could have helped while he was away. Wagon trains were coming from all over, St. Louis primarily, and passing through Salt Lake City on their way to the gold fields in California.

"The people had money, if they got that far with their wagons," I stated.

I saw the mischief in Dad's eyes, the grin working up, his mind processing the best answer. The right one.

"So why did Parley go broke on the tollroad?"

"No quarters," Dad answered with a straight face.

"What do you mean, 'no quarters'?"

"Parley forgot when he built the roads," he answered.

"Forgot?"

"The quarters," he smiled. "You ever been on a tollroad in this country that didn't take quarters? He forgot to ask for quarters."

We had a good laugh. But it was as good an answer as any for the Pratts' string of financial misadventures.

"Dad, I did some research and found the original

plat map of downtown Salt Lake City. Do you know where Grandpa Parley's lot was? The one Brigham Young assigned to him?"

"No, Son. Where was it?" he asked, still grinning. He really didn't know, but if it was downtown property it would be worth many millions in today's currency.

"The Marriott. The Marriott Hotel, Dad! When we stay in the Marriott downtown, we are staying on family land."

"Well, I'll be a son of a gun," he said, shaking his head. "Well, the Pratts have always sold out cheap, but when you give a man your word, you've just got to keep it."

"Seems to me like we should be hiring an attorney. You know, just in case there's some legal recourse."

We were both having fun with the truth. "Buy high, sell low," seemed to be a well established Pratt real estate credo. At least it's always worked that way with me.

It's been many years since that conversation took place, and Dad has long since left us. But just a month or so ago I got an email.

"Are you the son of Grant Pratt?" the man asked.

"Yes, I am," I typed back.

"My name is Don Pratt. We are distant cousins." Then he went on to remind me how the two of us had met some thirty years earlier at a small junior college in California and compared family trees. I vaguely remembered, but what was most important came out in the following lines:

"I just want to tell you that you should be very honored. We are now living in Simi Valley, the place where you grew up."

"Thank you," I answered. "Yes, Simi Valley was home."

"I get asked all the time if I am one of Grant Pratt's sons. You should know that to a person, whenever I am asked, the person goes on about how honest your dad was and what a kind man he was. The power of the name is still very strong here."

I swallowed hard as I read the email. I replied that I was truly touched and grateful that I had been the son of a man so well-respected and loved, and thanked him for the good news — that the name was alive and well back home.

"It's been over twenty years since he lived there," I added.

"People haven't forgotten," he finished.

I sat there at the computer, recalling Dad's unique voice, remembering his telling me something that at the time seemed quite ordinary but had now become very significant. I smiled, realizing the Pratts were wealthy after all. In my mind's eye, I could still see his grin, then hear the clear, quiet voice:

Remember, Son — There's no substitute for a good name.

CHAPTER 8

AN HONEST DAY'S WORK FOR AN HONEST DAY'S PAY

Dad believed work to be a moral duty, an imperative. To work, and to do work well was the measure of a man.

"Always give the man you work for an honest day's work for an honest day's pay, and then give a little bit more, and you will never be out of a job." He had told us boys this many times, and my oldest brother, Grant Jr., recently reminded me of it during a long-distance telephone call.

The counsel is wise of course. The successful scholar knows that his or her best effort, plus a little more, is A+ work. The Olympic athlete who wins the gold medal by a fraction of a second, achieves the honor by giving his or her best, plus a little more. Winners in business understand the difference it makes when they extend themselves to satisfy the customer or provide an additional service. All these are winners precisely because they not only do not complain about work, but actually perform what is required and then do a little more.

Dad believed that it was the first duty of every man to take care of the woman he married and the children of that marriage. For most of his life, he honored that commitment by doing hard, physical labor. Questioned about his ability to put in long days, shoveling, hauling, lifting, building, he would often say, "Hard work never killed anyone."

I debated that statement with Dad a few times. I actually think hard work *has* killed a lot of people. You know, in accidents caused by exhaustion, where the worker becomes careless or literally succumbs to fatigue.

"Electrocuted, Dad. I'll bet someone, somewhere, worked so hard they forgot something and, battazing, they stuck their hand somewhere it wasn't supposed to be and got killed. I'll bet ya."

"Oh . . ." he'd say, and then get flustered, as he

always did whenever I'd tease him about one of his sayings.

"Look, Dad. Why do you think there is something called OSHA? Because people kill themselves working too hard. And what about all the federal and state agencies that regulate the workplace? And the labor unions and all their rules, designed especially to protect the worker. Dad, work *can* kill."

"Oh, why don't you go to law school?" he would counter, mildly perturbed, knowing that I had a point but not wanting to be sidetracked.

But deep inside I believed him. Down deep I understood what he meant when he said "hard work never killed anyone." Held by him and those of his generation, that was the attitude that had rescued the world from the economic ruin of the 1930's worldwide financial crash and hauled it out of the wreckage of World War II.

Hard work not only builds muscle, it also builds character and bolsters confidence. If a man can go through a day, shoulder to shoulder with any other man, then give just a bit more, he knows he's equal to any task and that he'll likely never be out of a job.

What made Dad special was that he wasn't only able to endure hard work, he *loved* hard work. Hard, physical labor defined him — as it did many of the men his age.

They had grown up during the Great Depression. It was "great," not because it was something wonderful, but because of its depth and duration. Lasting more than a decade, it consumed not only this nation's wealth but also the world's. Today we call these downturns in the economy *recessions*. But no recession has matched the economic depression of the 1930s. It touched virtually everyone, and the hardships it caused had a profound effect on anyone who lived through it.

Those hard times required families and friends to pull together in order to just keep themselves fed, clothed, and housed, and it wasn't uncommon for people to work twelve-hour days, six and seven days a week. Jobs were hard to come by, and people who had work did not complain. From what Dad has told me, everyone was in the same boat, and they learned to help each other. The prevailing attitude was: "Everything is up from here."

Working two, even three, jobs at times, Dad and

his peers laughed, joked, and enjoyed themselves as much or more than those of the present generation who wonder what kind of "signing bonus" they will get with their first "real job" out of college. Dad's generation didn't wait for the signing bonus. They didn't understand what an "entitlement program" was. They didn't expect unemployment benefits. There was no welfare plan or safety net of any kind. They simply did their best at their work, trade, or job, and then did a little more.

The generation that entered the Great Depression as children helped bring about its end. Ask your dad or grandfather what it was like. If he lived through it, you may see a furrowed brow, hear a sigh, and witness a shake of the head. "Those were hard times, you understand," he might say. Then watch for the twinkle in his eye. Memory has a funny way of smoothing out the rough spots. You will likely hear stories of pranks, the delight taken in simple, homespun pleasures, the joy that accompanied receiving even a small gift for Christmas, and a certain pride that he survived the hardships.

Deprived as they were, those hearty souls

wouldn't be extinguished. A spark remained, and out of their want and hard work came the greatest prosperity in all of recorded history! The economic growth that occurred in many parts of the world during the last sixty years of the twentieth century was unprecedented, making luxuries, conveniences, and comforts available to common people that kings of earlier ages couldn't even have imagined.

Dad was one of those who endured, learned to be content with what little he had, worked hard to earn a living for his family, and finally saw the end of hard times.

Your dad or grandfather, who lived in those times, would likely say: "You kids would have had to have been there to understand." He might add: "I wouldn't want to do it again." But then he would most certainly conclude, " . . . but I wouldn't trade the experience for the world."

So it was good, hard-earned advice that Dad gave me and his other six sons:

Always give the man who employs you just a little bit more than he pays you for, and you'll never be out of a job.

CHAPTER 9

"IMITATE THE CARPENTER: MEASURE TWICE, CUT ONCE"

"I mitate the carpenter," Dad would tell me, "measure twice, cut once. It's easier to make it right in the beginning than to fix it in the end."

During his retirement to an old country home in Idaho, Dad enjoyed working in a shop in his barn-like garage. There, he turned out a variety of carefully crafted wooden creations — mostly small pieces of furniture. And the best rocking horses sold anywhere, I'm proud to add.

He also created fun things, puzzles, the type of mind-challenging toys that took far more time to produce than he could ever sell for a profit. On my desk sits a block of wood that easily fits in the palm of my hand. It is carefully sanded with the inside scooped out in an "L" shape and has a small, black wood tack pressed into the soft pine, so that the tack is sitting as if it has a roof over its head. On this keepsake from my Dad are the hand-painted words: "Tack's Shelter."

He sometimes recovered the cost when he sold his work, but mostly he gave the handmade creations away. His aim wasn't to make money. "It's to make other people happy," he'd say.

Although naturally shy as a boy and as a young man, in his later years Dad ended up being a good speaker in church and other public meetings. But the way he lived his life are the sermons people recall today. In his treatment of others, he tried to emulate the Carpenter of Nazareth. He would often remind me that if a man did that, he could never go wrong.

"How many beams do you think He crafted, Son? Over the course of his youth and adult life, working with Joseph in Nazareth, how many beams for building houses do you think Jesus made, helped erect?"

"Quite a few, I suppose."

"Strange, isn't it, that He made wooden beams

for a livelihood, and that in the end He was nailed to a wooden beam. I wonder what He thought?"

I was stunned by the idea. Another carpenter, one in Jerusalem, with his plane, in his shop, would shave rough beams for a cross, then supply them to the Romans for the execution. And to one such beam, the Master Carpenter, the Son of God, would be cruelly nailed.

How ironic. That a wooden beam such as he had fashioned so many times with His own hands, should one day receive the nails that pierced those hands. Given Jesus' growing awareness of His mission and the awful events that would lead to His death, it must have crossed His mind that he would give His life on a wooden cross, shaped by another man's hands. The irony held me as spellbound then as it does now.

"So He understands us after all," I said.

"I suppose He does," Dad answered.

Dad took pride in his handiwork and felt the Lord honored the honest work men and women do with their hands. Dad simply did his best to imitate the Master Carpenter, not wanting to give the recipients of his work anything less than his personal best from his shop.

Dad wasn't unusual in wanting to do that. It's a common thing for a man to want to do his best, especially when his work is going to be on public display. But taking pride in what he created provided a great example for me—that honest work is worthwhile and the care we take in what we do is an extension of our character. That is why Dad took care to make sure to leave no detail undone. The edges of his creations were always smoothed, so no child or adult would ever get a splinter. The components of stools, chairs, rocking horses, and the puzzles, all fit perfectly.

Why? Because his work carried his name and his love to its recipient. He delivered more than carefully crafted work out of his small carpenter's shop on 20th Street in Heyburn, Idaho. Those pieces also carried a message.

I'm not sure Dad gave much conscious thought to his work being a message. But whenever any of us received one of his finely crafted toys or a piece of carefully finished furniture (which Mom also enjoyed helping him build) the gift really said: "Here it is. Not much, but my best. I love you."

Simple. Straightforward. The look of joy and pride on his face when each of us would inspect his work was obvious. It was pay enough.

His tools mostly sit idle nowadays. Used only occasionally by one of the younger sons or Mom, they stand waiting for the carpenter to return. But I'm sure if he could, he'd be turning out handy items to decorate his friends' and family members' homes, gifts to brighten their lives. Those he created and disbursed remain as silent testimony to what he taught us so well:

Imitate the carpenter: measure twice, cut once.

CHAPTER 10

"DON'T WORRY ABOUT THINGS YOU CAN'T DO ANYTHING ABOUT..."

S on, don't worry about things you can't do anything about, and don't worry about things you
can." That was the advice Dad gave me when I was
going through a particularly difficult and trying time.

It was the winter of 1976, and I was about to
turn twenty-three years old. I had been worried
about my Dad's struggling business and the atten-
dant financial stress that was weighing my parents
down and had come home from college to help
them. At the same time, I was searching to know
what to do with my personal life and suffering from
some severe chronic pain that was keeping me
fatigued and discouraged.

I had really wanted to attend college, be with

friends, date, and enjoy those fleeting years of youth. But the only way I was going to be able to pay for my education was to use one of the military scholarships offered by Army ROTC. I enrolled, took the oath to uphold the Constitution of the United States, got my shots, and set out to make up the first two years I'd already missed, by enrolling in a training program the Army offered at Fort Knox, Kentucky—ironically, the same military camp where my father had started and ended his military adventure some thirty-one years earlier, during World War II.

The ROTC camp wasn't scheduled to begin until July, so as soon as school was out for the summer, I found work in Washington D.C. and took a room with six other young men in a rented house in Annandale, Virginia. I was happy to be able to see our nation's capital, earn a little money, and be near the exciting place where the decisions affecting our citizens were being made. I was thinking I might even enjoy a career in the military and be able to work at the Pentagon one day or on a military post nearby.

I had some great housemates, and it was a good

situation where I was able to prepare my mind and body to undergo two months of army basic training in the humidity of the Midwest. I exercised and ran daily through the dense forest trails abundant in Northern Virginia and tried to gear myself to endure the rigors of military training—obeying orders, carrying a heavy pack on dead runs, crawling in the mud, fighting sleep on all-night training exercises, and participating in general military drills.

That was what I had planned to do, but what kept nagging at me was knowing what my parents were going through—putting in long, six-day weeks and enduring tremendous physical and emotional hardships as they struggled to provide for themselves. I knew from actual experience Dad routinely loaded and unloaded truckloads of heavy goods, by hand, and I was torn between my desire to get an education and the guilt I felt for not helping them with their work at our family-owned retail store.

As a boy, I had seen Dad's anxiety during the hard winter months, when construction work sometimes slowed, and particularly during a couple of economic slowdowns in the 1960s. I had pledged then that when I grew up I would take care of my parents and make sure they never had to worry financially again. I had been so proud of my older brothers, Grant and Nick, who even while serving in Vietnam during the war, often sent their pay home to our folks. Then, after they were married and had families of their own to take care of, they continued to help out as much as they could. I felt it my duty to follow their good example.

That youthful promise I had made haunted me now. I prayed to know what to do. I wanted to get an education and find ways to give expression to my creative talents and have a broader life experience than I thought I could get by losing my college years to work in a small, insignificant country store.

If I accepted the military scholarship, it would mean making a commitment that would keep me from ever returning to the help that I had been in my father's business. I would not be able to relieve him during the hard hours, nor work at his side. If I left school and continued going piecemeal as I had been — going off to school for a semester, staying and working by his side for a semester — then I would probably not finish school for many years. And I would miss many of the social and other pleasant aspects of college life that come only once in a young life. I would also not serve my country in uniform as I had always assumed I would, and I would likely hurt my future family by failing to make adequate preparation for a career.

After agonizing over the choices, I decided to put my education and military career on hold, to answer a greater call I felt to father, mother, and family.

So, instead of driving my 1970 Chevy Impala from the nation's capitol and parking it in the enlisted men's parking lot off Fort Knox, Kentucky, I drove cross-country to the Pacific Coast and back to Simi Valley where I threw in with my fifty-seven-year-old dad in his struggle to make a go of the family enterprise.

It was during those days that turned into weeks, then months, that I really got to know my parents but more especially Dad. That was a plus, but it was hard emotionally, and it was hard physically. I spent my time driving a delivery truck and manually loading and unloading thousands of pounds of goods and also worrying about how to meet our obligations and eke out a profit. Besides, I was now twenty-three years old, and I felt it was time for me to consider marriage. The thoughts of all I had given up and where I was headed weighed heavily upon me. I was having my own summer of discontent.

After one particularly stressful business day, when revenue was down and the pressure to pay bills was up, and I was feeling especially frustrated, Dad said he was going to go into a small trailer we had parked behind our building and take a nap. We had finished the essential work of the day, and there was really nothing left to do but close up shop. But I was chafing under the pressure to find a way to fix things, make things better, get more customers through the door, and deal with the struggles of my personal life.

"Dad?"

"Yes, son?"

"How can you just go and take a nap? I mean, things are bad. They are tough. We need to make some more business, and I don't see how you can just brush it off, take a nap, and—"

"Son . . . listen to me," he said. "I'm going to tell you something my father told me long ago."

That got my attention. Although this book might lead you to believe Dad was always spouting off great wisdom, the soft-spoken man only occasionally gave me any direct advice. Most of what I learned from him was from his example. It wasn't until years later that I realized how much wisdom there was in the few words he so infrequently uttered.

So I perked up, was all ears. "Okay, Dad, I'm ready. What did Grandpa say?"

"Son, he said this to me: 'Don't worry about things you can't do anything about, and don't worry about things you can.'" He smiled, then, exhausted, he turned to walk away.

"Uh, Dad? Is that it?" I asked.

"Yep."

"So, I guess you are saying don't worry?"

He stopped and turned around. "Look, Son. Did we do our best today?"

"Yeah."

"Can we do any more to make it better?"

"Well, no, not really."

"So don't worry about things you can't do anything about. Simple, right?"

"Yeah," I acknowledged.

"And don't worry about the things you can."

I spent the rest of the day wrestling with the math of what he had said, before it made sense. But

I don't think there has been a day in the twenty-seven intervening years that his advice has not blessed and served me somehow.

It was there, working in that difficult business, away from where I wanted to be, that I learned the twelve extraordinary values in real time—the virtues I am sharing with you in this book.

Had I taken the military up on their offer, finished my degree at the university, I would have been satisfied and happy. My parents would have been proud. I would have served self, country, and others.

But under the guidance of a World War II corporal, his prospective second lieutenant son was unwittingly given this text. Now, a quarter of a century later, I understand what Dad had wanted his children to know about values such as honesty, wholesomeness, humor, kindness, work, selfless service. It sometimes hurts not to be able to show him the work that he created in me. But then he'd say, "Son, something my father told me long ago:

'Don't worry about things you can't do anything about, and don't worry about things you can.'"

CHAPTER 11

"THEY WERE JUST LIKE US . . ."

It didn't matter to Dad what the German prisoners believed. He knew what he believed, and that was all that really mattered. He saw them as men whose lives of war were now behind them.

Dad's First Armored Division was one of only two American divisions available in Europe (stationed in Ireland early in 1942) for the fight against the Nazis and their allies. These Americans were the men who would see fighting first, two years before the famed "D-Day" invasion on the beaches at Normandy, France. From these men came our country's first defeats and first victories against the German war machine, in North Africa and Italy.

Two years before men began dying for freedom

at Normandy, they had already been dying in North Africa, at places called Sidi-bou-Zid, Kasserine Pass, Gafsa, then in Sicily, and at Anzio, Salerno, and Monte Cassino in Italy. The lessons they learned there readied the Allied forces for the heralded invasion of June 6, 1944, so talked of, so hallowed in the memory of so many.

It was at the end of the fighting in North Africa in 1943. Dad and those with him were hardened veterans now, and they didn't know there was still more than a year of hellish fighting they couldn't even imagine ahead of them.

Dad was in charge of guarding a truckload of German soldiers, who were among tens of thousands of Germans who were walking in from the Tunisian desert to surrender. The beaten men were being gathered in huge open fields, POW camps, outside Bizerte, Tunisia.

"Wie geht's," one said.

"What is your name?" another said in English, pulling a photo from his pocket. "I'm Klaus. This is my family. My father, my mother, my sister. They send us to Amerika?"

Dad could see these men were done. They had

been tough fighters, had run the Americans into the ground just the year before at Kasserine Pass. No doubt some of these men had been there shooting at him. But they had finally lost their war, and they knew it. Two years in the harsh African desert, being driven by the English from the east and the Americans from the west, strafed by American and British fighter planes, no supplies, no relief, ordered by Berlin to fight to the death . . .

Dad saw they were ready for American hospitality. These men knew how the Americans would treat them. They were, in a word, *happy* to be out of the war. Dad said he had envied them. He knew they would indeed be treated humanely and with fairness. He knew there would be no more terror from the artillery, no more strafing from planes diving upon them unexpectedly, no more bitter and hungry days and nights, waiting for death in some foxhole. Ordinary men, not supermen as the propaganda had made them out to be, they looked like guys he knew—same age, same tired eyes.

"So I set my Thompson submachine gun on the truck bench next to me and pulled out my wallet and shared a photo of Mom in a one-piece bathing suit."

"Dad," I protested, "what if one of them had grabbed the gun?"

He chuckled and shook his head. "No, Son. They were just like me. They were happy to be out of the fight. Where would they go? No, they wanted nothing more to do with the fighting. I knew my war was going to continue, but these guys were out of it, and they were glad."

He recalled how they were soon all laughing and sharing photos of their "girls back home."

Dad could see that, draftees, like himself, the Germans were sons of the same God as he was, who just wanted out of the mess they were in. How he was able to view them that way in light of all the destruction and torment their leaders had caused was revealing and has stayed with me.

The fact is, Dad knew that the armies clashing for control of territory in order to win a battle were made up of ordinary young men—city boys, farm boys, factory workers, grocers, students, shop-keeper's sons—boys and men who had families. Meeting them face to face had debunked the notion that Hitler had propagated, that they possessed mythical powers and were members of a warrior super race.

Dad escorted the truck of jovial prisoners to the barbed wire enclosure and then set out in the empty truck to get a fresh load of the "enemy," now weaponless, and walking in from desert outposts.

He had retold the story to me several times, and I wondered why it meant so much to him. He came home from the war with a realization that he and his fellow soldiers had indeed participated in the greatest military conflict in history — they had saved the planet from the forces of evil.

But the evil was in Berlin and Tokyo and in perhaps some enemy soldiers' hearts who knew hate and not the peace that kindness brings.

"Can you fire a weapon at someone when you have that kind of understanding, Dad? You were religious. How did you do it?"

"Oh, they were shooting at us, and I was just a soldier. We were doing our duty, nothing personal. We all understood that, and we knew that the enemy had a gun to their backs to fight us. We saw the soldiers for what they were and knew Hitler was another kind of evil. So we just did our duty and were glad to get it over."

After the North Africa campaign, Dad went on to fight in Italy, in some of the worst battles of the war. He endured the ferocious battle for Anzio, that four-month torture our forces lived in on a beachhead above Naples and south of Rome.

The First Armored Division went into Rome on June 6, 1944, D-Day at Normandy, France, a thousand miles plus to the north and west. They had already been at war against the Germans since the fall of 1942. By this time the American Army had gained strength, battle experience, and knowledge of how to fight the enemy that had vowed to conquer all of Europe and then the world.

Dad's best friend died during the battle for Anzio. I saw the painful memories written on his face as he said, "He was going to be a rancher in Montana when he got home. A German 88 gun got him. Direct hit on his truck. He burned to death."

"Did you hate the Germans after that, Dad?"

"No. They were stuck there doing their job, just like us."

"Were you ever afraid?"

"At Anzio we would dig deeper every day, and the shells still came. They say we lost more men on that beach than MacArthur lost in all his Pacific campaigns. Yeah, I was afraid. I cried. We all cried. We just never knew if the next one would be the end."

"You cried?" I asked in amazement, thinking by then, somehow, a soldier got used to war's vagaries, the shelling, the uncertainties, the strafing and bombing, death.

"Yeah," he said and looked away. "We were scared."

I was at Dad's side the moment of his death. I reminded him of those war stories he had told me over the years. He couldn't speak, but his eyes glistened as he listened and as he labored for breath. I read his eulogy to him minutes before he closed his eyes for the final time. I included this story of his friend, all his friends who went with him to Africa and Italy to do their part to "save the planet." And then I added:

"And, Dad? I'm going to tell every one at the memorial service about those German prisoners who came in from the desert. How you treated them with kindness. I'm going to tell them, Dad, that they were sons of God, just like us."

His eyes grew wide and with a slight nod of his head, he approved. A light squeeze of my hand, and his tired, tear-filled eyes told me he was just a soldier yesterday, learning valor, courage under fire, and kindness. That knowledge was what he brought home from the war . . .

Son, they were just like us. Sons of the same God.

CHAPTER 12

THE THREE MOST POWERFUL WORDS

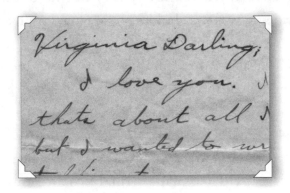

Virginia Darling,
I love you. I
thats about all I
but I wanted to wr
t li t

"Express love while you can. It's who you are in here," he said, pointing to my chest, "and in the end, that's the only thing that matters."

Words are symbols of the action implied in them. Dad was more a man of action than words, yet his final words summed up the man.

He was unable to speak during his last week of life. He had elected to die with dignity in his small Idaho farm home, and my deaf mother could only helplessly watch as he gasped for air during those final days, unwilling to leave until he was invited by a Higher Power. My sister, who lived next door to them, finally called and told me to hurry from my home in Utah, four hours away. Hoping this was really not the end, I asked her to tell him to wait for me. Then I delayed my trip until the following morning. I was selfish. I knew he would wait, and I didn't want him to go.

He suffered through that entire night and into the middle of the next day, a devoted father keeping his word. What I saw as I walked into the room shocked me. Even more skeletal than two weeks before, and fighting for air, he relaxed as I entered the room. He had made a final promise and had kept it.

He spoke to me with his eyes as I sat beside him and read to him the eulogy I had prepared. I sought his approval. Unable to speak, he just weakly nodded his head.

Grant Pratt was a religious man and a spiritual man. You can be one or the other or both. He was both. His most fervent desires were that his children share his belief in God, and that we understand that our dad loved us.

By then, it was physically impossible for him to speak. His voice was gone, his lungs rattled, and his breathing was labored and shallow.

I wanted him to witness to me one more time

that there is a God. I needed to hear it from him. So I asked a question. I asked it for both him and myself, knowing he would somehow answer.

"Dad?" I asked.

He stirred in an attempt to keep his tired eyes open.

"Is Jesus Christ the Son of God?"

He groaned as if he would shout, and his back arched as if he would rise from his bed if he could. "Don't you know that by now?" his face questioned, appealing to me to believe. Then he relaxed.

I was stunned at the great final physical exertion he made. I had my answer and was satisfied. I felt this was all I would get from Dad by way of communication. I had given him an opportunity to testify, and he had given one last gift to me—his final testimony. *What I wouldn't do for one more hour of talking with him,* I said silently.

It was time for him to leave. The talking was finished.

Mom said a tearful good-bye as she stroked his head and kissed him over and over, whispering into his ear, "You can go now, Grant. You can go, darling."

My father groaned, struggling to form something with his lips, but unable to do so. He could barely raise an eyelid now but kept trying to speak, at least with his eyes. Even if he had been able to speak to his wife, her deafness would have prevented her from receiving the offering.

He closed his moist eyes and tears drained from their corners as his pulse steadily weakened. I sat at his side holding his left hand with both of mine.

So this is how Dad dies. Congratulations, Dad, I found myself thinking. He had "finished the race" and had "fought the good fight," as Paul the ancient apostle wrote.

I didn't expect any more from Dad. But suddenly he turned his head to me, and he opened his eyes once again. Gazing intently into mine he said in the clearest and most deliberate earthly voice he had ever owned, these words—"I love you"—and then his eyes closed, and he was gone.

In the end it won't matter what is left behind, if the gift of love isn't. The three most powerful words any father or parent can speak to his child, and any child can speak to his parent were his final words, his parting gift to me. Of all the sacred words in human language, they are the three that say it all.

He didn't leave a famous name. He left no money or wealth. But I was given something most kids on the block never got. He left me with his heart and soul, and that's not bad. And after all, my dad was a hero. He had lied to save the planet, and that's something no one can take away . . .

Express your love while time is on your side. In the end, it will be the only thing that matters.

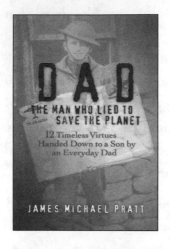

DAD
THE MAN WHO LIED TO SAVE THE PLANET

12 Timeless Virtues Handed Down to a Son by an Everyday Dad

JAMES MICHAEL PRATT

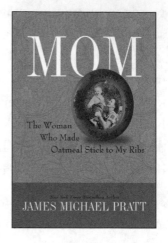

MOM
The Woman Who Made Oatmeal Stick to My Ribs

New York Times Bestselling Author

JAMES MICHAEL PRATT

THE BELOVED *NEW YORK TIMES* BESTSELLER

"A return ticket to *Bridges of Madison County* territory." —*People*

The Last Valentine

James Michael Pratt

The Innkeeper's Gift

Summer 2004

Order other novels by
James Michael Pratt

Dad: The Man Who Lied to Save The Planet - $6.95
Mom: The Woman Who Made Oatmeal Stick to My Ribs - $6.95
The Last Valentine - $6.95
The Innkeeper's Gift - $6.95

Mail check or money order to:
Apricot Press   P.O. Box 1611
American Fork, Utah   84003

Credit card orders call:
801-756-0456

Allow 3 weeks for delivery

Quantity discounts available
Call for more information
9 a.m. - 5 p.m. MST

To find out more about his writing,
his Book Club, novels, upcoming work,
and his personal appearances nationwide,
visit him at www.jmpratt.com.